The Behavior of U.S. Export Prices and Profit Margins, 1981-1986

Office of Trade and Investment Analysis
International Trade Administration
U.S. Department of Commerce

The Behavior of U.S. Export Prices and Profit Margins, 1981-1986

Office of Trade and Investment Analysis
International Trade Administration
U.S. Department of Commerce

ISBN: 0-87186-341-3 (paperback)   89-12152

First printing in bound-book form: 1988
First printed in the United States of America

PRICE: $3.50

COMMITTEE FOR ECONOMIC DEVELOPMENT
477 Madison Avenue, New York, N.Y. 10022 / (212) 688-2063
1700 K Street, N.W., Washington, D.C. 20006 / (202) 296-5860

CONTENTS

<u>TEXT</u> <u>FIGURES</u>

FOREWORD

This paper, <u>The Behavior of U.S. Export Prices and Profit Margins, 1981-1986</u>, was researched and written by Victoria L. Hatter of the U.S. Department of Commerce.

The Committee for Economic Development (CED) is publishing this paper as a public service to make it available to those working on issues relevant to U.S.-Japan economic relations. This paper is an analytical document and should not be construed as a statement of U.S. Department of Commerce or CED policy.

CED is an independent, nonprofit, and nonpartisan organization comprised of 250 corporate and academic leaders. Our members actively develop policy analysis and recommendations by blending their practical experience and background knowledge with the research capabilities of expert economists and social scientists.

CED, in collaboration with its Japanese counterpart organization, Keizai Doyukai (the Japan Association of Corporate Executives), has been studying various aspects of U.S.-Japanese economic relations for a number of years. The latest joint project of the two organizations is developing a semi-annual bulletin on U.S. and Japanese trade and economic developments.

Additional copies of the following paper can be ordered from CED in New York at (212) 688-2063. Questions on the content of the paper should be directed to Victoria L. Hatter at (202) 377-3895.

Robert C. Holland
President
Committee for Economic Development

THE BEHAVIOR OF U.S. EXPORT PRICES AND PROFIT MARGINS, 1981-1986

EXECUTIVE SUMMARY AND KEY FINDINGS

The main objective of this study was to examine the behavior of U.S. dollar export prices and profit margins for manufactures products for the period 1981-1986. The study attempts to determine:

1. when the dollar was appreciating between 1981 and early 1985, did U.S. exporters reduce prices and/or profit margins in order to try to maintain their price competitiveness in international markets?; and,

2. after the dollar began to depreciate in early 1985, did U.S. exporters raise prices/profit margins, thus allowing only part of the potential improvement in price competitiveness to occur?

The key findings of the study are:

During the dollar appreciation period (1981-1985:Q1)

o   Dollar export prices rose for more than two-thirds of the products surveyed. On average, prices rose by about 15 percent during the period. These price increases, on top of the 25 percent real appreciation of the dollar, probably contributed to a significant reduction in the international price competitiveness of U.S. exports.

o   Only one-third of the products showed significant declines in estimated profit margins. Thus, it would appear that the pricing policies of U.S. exporters were more closely tied to profits than to maintaining market share in foreign countries.

o   Some of the products which did show definite declines in profit margins were inorganic chemicals, paper, nonferrous metals, hand tools, ADP equipment, and electronic components.

During the dollar depreciation period (1985:Q1-1986)

o   Export prices for about half of the products rose dur[i]
this period. Although price changes varied widely am[o]
the individual products, on average, prices for all th[e]
included products rose by about 5.5 percent. Thus, a[.]
one-quarter of the potential benefit of the more than
percent real depreciation of the dollar was offset by
price increases.

o   As might be expected, decreases in profit margins --
which occurred for only one-third of the products when
the dollar was strong -- were less frequent after the
dollar began to weaken. For the vast majority of
products, profit margins were unchanged or increased.

o   Among the products where profit margins increased were
organic and inorganic chemicals, paper, textiles, and
electric motors.

INTRODUCTION

Despite the sharp decline in the foreign exchange value of the dollar against the Japanese yen and most major European currencies since early 1985, the United States has continued to run a very large deficit in its manufactures trade. The 1986 deficit reached nearly $129 billion, an increase of $27 billion over 1985. The failure of U.S. exports to expand rapidly in response to the dollar's depreciation and the presumed resultant improvement in export price competitiveness has contributed to the continued rise in the trade deficit. Even though U.S. manufactures exports grew by nearly 7 percent in 1986 from their 1985 level, much faster than in recent years, the 1986 total of $179.9 billion was only slightly higher than the previous 1981 peak.

There are several possible reasons why U.S. exports have been slow to respond to the dollar's recent depreciation. First, it is expected that there would be some lag between the time the dollar began to depreciate and the time foreign buyers recognize, or can react to the change in relative prices. Furthermore, changes in relative prices may not be sufficient to encourage purchases if foreign economies are not expanding rapidly enough to stimulate increased demand for U.S. exports. Finally, structural shifts in U.S. industry may have occurred during the dollar appreciation period which have contributed to the stagnation in U.S. manufactures exports after the dollar began to depreciate.

The expectation of improved exports resulting from the recent exchange rate changes presupposes that dollar depreciation has resulted in a favorable change in relative prices between U.S. exports and our major competitors' exports. However, a favorable change in relative prices may not have occurred if U.S. exporters have raised their dollar prices and thus not allowed all, or a significant part, of the fall in the dollar's value to be reflected in lower foreign currency prices for U.S. exports. In addition, if a competitor's currency has not changed relative to the dollar, as is the case for many developing countries, then the U.S. exporter does not gain any price advantage via exchange rates.

The purpose of this paper is to explore the behavior of U.S. export prices between 1981 and 1986, with particular attention to the period after early 1985 when the dollar began to depreciate against major industrial country currencies. If U.S. exporters held dollar prices steady after early 1985, so that the improved price competitiveness effects of the dollar devaluation have been wholly or significantly realized, then the explanation for the slow growth in U.S. exports and the failure of the U.S. trade deficit to improve may be attributable to other factors.

The paper is divided into three parts. The first part summarizes the general approach, the rationale for that approach, and the methodological details. The second part analyzes the results of the study, and the third contains the summary and conclusions.

GENERAL BACKGROUND

PURPOSES

The purpose of this paper is to explore the behavior of U.S. expo
prices during two time periods: between 1981 and early 1985 when
dollar appreciated by about 25 percent in real terms and, betweer
early 1985 and year end 1986 when the dollar depreciated by about
percent in real terms. Two questions will be addressed:

1. When the dollar was appreciating, did U.S. exporters
minimize dollar price increases or even lower dollar prices
an attempt to lessen the adverse price competitiveness effe
in order to maintain market shares?

2. During the dollar depreciation period, did U.S. exporte
refrain from raising dollar prices and thus allow all or mo
of the price competitiveness advantage to be realized?

In addition, the study explores the behavior of the profit margin
of U.S exporters during both the dollar appreciation period and t
dollar depreciation period to provide additional information as t
how U.S. exporters have reacted to exchange rate changes. In
particular, were pricing patterns of U.S. exporters more responsi
to changes in market share or changes in profit margins? Two
questions were addressed:

1. When the dollar was appreciating, did U.S. exporters red
profit margins in order to maintain price competitiveness
thus preserve market shares?

2. Since the dollar began to depreciate, have U.S. exporter
increased profit margins, thus possibly negating, at least
partially, the positive price competitive effects of that
depreciation?

The ability to offset a strengthening dollar by holding steady or
reducing dollar export prices is necessarily limited by the need
make a profit and also since selling below cost (dumping) is ille
under GATT. For example, when the dollar is appreciating, if an
exporter raises prices, but by less than any increase in producti
costs, then his profit margins will fall. This would indicate th
he may be trying to minimize the worsening in relative price
competitiveness. In contrast, when the dollar is depreciating, i
an exporter allows his price to fall, but his production costs are
declining faster, then he is sacrificing a part of the potential
gain in price competitiveness in order to expand his profit
margins.

METHODOLOGY

Export Prices -- Unit values were calculated to be used as proxies for actual export prices. However, the detailed Schedule E commodity unit values were supplemented by actual export price data from the Bureau of Labor Statistics for more aggregated commodities where the Census data were inadequate or unavailable. Quarterly UVI data were calculated for the period 1981 through the third quarter of 1986. the fourth quarter of 1986 is based on the average of October-November data.

A few cautionary words regarding the export UVI and price data are in order:

- o   Despite the high level of commodity disaggregation, the possibility remains that changes in the UVIs reflect changes in composition as well as price.

- o   The UVIs cannot be adjusted to take account of quality changes and upscaling. (The BLS export price data do attempt to account for these type of changes.) Thus, assuming quality improvements and/or upscaling, UVI decreases (increases) understate (overstate) price changes.

- o   The BLS export price data may, in some cases, reflect list prices rather than transactions prices.

Profit Margins -- Changes in profit margins between two periods in time were determined by comparing the actual change in export unit values/prices with the change required to hold profit margins constant. It was assumed that profit margins would be unchanged if the dollar export price was raised (lowered) by the same percentage as cost of producing that product rose (fell). Wholesale price indexes (WPIs) were used to approximate production costs. Profit margin indexes were calculated by taking the ratio of export unit value indexes (UVIs) relative to wholesale price indexes (WPIs).

A cautionary word about the interpretation of profit margins is in order. Given that the profit margin indexes only provide an approximation of the changes in profit margins, only indexes that change substantially should be viewed as evidence of changes in profit margins. To give a notional range, indexes that show less than a 5 percent change are probably best considered as indicating little or no change in profit margins.

In order to estimate changes in profit margins, it was necessary to find a proxy for production costs. Wholesale prices were chosen for this purpose, specifically, the producer price indexes published by the Bureau of Labor Statistics. Since the export unit value/price data and the producer price index data are classified by two different classification systems, it was impossible to assure perfect comparability between them. However, export UVI/BLS pric product groups were matched as closely as possible with similar producer price product groups.

Product Coverage -- Specific commodities were chosen to represent broader commodity groups. The value of exports and the comparability of product classes over time were the major considerations in the selection process. Because of the large number of individual U.S. export commodities -- more than 4,600 Schedule E classifications at the most detailed (7-digit) level - and the unmanageability of such a large database -- it was necess to severely restrict the product sample.

To be considered for inclusion in the product sample, a 7-digit S E export product class must have had a value of exports of at lea $100 million for any year 1983--1985 or Jan.-Oct. 1986. This val cutoff was made for two reasons: first, we wanted to cover as lar a portion of total export value as possible while keeping the si of the database manageable; and second, the larger the export val for a particular commodity group, the greater the likelihood that the frequency and mix of shipments for a specific product class would be stable over time. This would mean that changes in unit values would reflect price changes rather than shifts in product composition.

About 167 Sch. E commodities were initially selected for inclusi in the product sample. The initial number of categories was increased by the addition of several product categories from the Bureau of Labor Statistics export price series where the coverage for a large commodity area was inadequate or unavailable from the Census data. For example, parts of various types of machinery ar important export items but unit values are generally not useable since units are often reported by weight (if at all). In order t fill this gap, BLS export price series were included for several categories of machinery parts and for several other product area The data were then screened for consistency of each item over tim As a result, the list of commodities included in the survey were reduced to 130 7-digit Sch. E classes and 25 BLS export price classes. These detailed products were then aggregated into approximately 40 broader product groups for analysis.

Though the final sample for major manufactures product categorie includes a substantial amount of exports in terms of dollar value and often accounts for a sizable share of total U.S. exports in product category, there is no assurance that the sample accurate reflects price movements for total U.S. exports in that product group. The 1985 value of exports for products included in the sample totalled $98.2 billion and represented nearly 60 percent o U.S. manufactures exports in that year. The coverage by major product class ranged from a low of 32 percent in basic manufactu to a high of 85 percent in transport equipment.

RESULTS

OVERVIEW

Export prices for three of the five broad commodity groups covered
here were higher at the peak of the dollar's appreciation (1985:1)
than in early 1981 (Figure 1). It should be noted, however, that
there was often considerable disparity in price movements among the
individual products included in each broad group. Nevertheless, the
broad groups whose included products are generally thought to be
more "unique" (transport equipment, machinery, miscellaneous
manufactures) showed increases in export prices during the dollar
appreciation period. In contrast, those broad groups with products
generally considered less differentiated (chemicals and basic
manufactures) showed little price change during the dollar
appreciation period. This difference in pricing patterns was not
unexpected given that the more homogenous the product, the less
latitude there generally is for differential pricing among competing
suppliers.

Figure 1

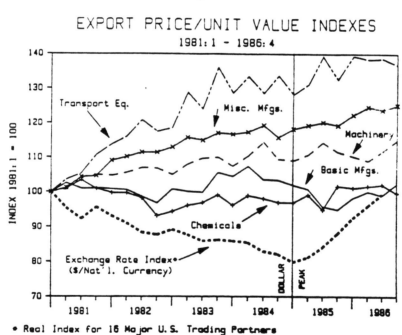

EXPORT PRICE/UNIT VALUE INDEXES
1981:1 - 1986:4

* Real Index for 16 Major U.S. Trading Partners

The pattern displayed during the dollar appreciation period
generally continued after the dollar began to depreciate in early
1985. Export prices for transport equipment, machinery, and
miscellaneous manufactures (dominated by instruments), continued to
increase. While export prices of basic manufactures and chemicals
also rose slightly, they remained close to their levels of early
1981.

Profit margins were not calculated for the broad overall groups since the necessary data were not available for all included individual products. Where available, profit margins are discus in the following individual product sections.

CHEMICALS

Product Sample

As shown in Table CHEM-1, the number of commodities included for chemicals was 43. These commodities, all of them 7-digit Sch. E product categories, accounted for one-third of all U.S. exports chemicals in 1985. One large valued chemicals product area, fertilizers, was not represented in this survey due to unavailability of sufficient time series for either unit values export prices.

Table CHEM-1

Profile of Product Sample

Product 1/	Number of Products in Sample	1985 Sample Value and % of Samp. Total		Sample Share of Total U.S Exports o: Product (%
		$ mill.	(%)	
Chemicals, total (5)	43	$7,300.0	(100)	33.5%
Organics (51)	18	$2,792.2	(38)	46.4%
Inorganics (52)	5	$ 737.3	(10)	22.5%
Plastics (58)	12	$2,001.0	(27)	53.0%
Other chemicals	8	$1,769.5	(24)	20.4%

1/ Product names are shortened versions of the full Sch. E descriptions. The Sch. E category's numeric designation represented by the products in the sample is shown in parentheses.

Note: Totals may not add due to rounding.

Price and Profit Margin Behavior

Overall, chemical prices increased very modestly between 1981 and 1984, declined in 1985 and then rose slightly. The overall patte however, masked significant differences in price as well as in profit margin behavior among the individual commodities (Table CHEM-2).

Dollar Appreciation Period, 1981-early 1985 -- The behavior of prices and profit margins varied widely among the major chemical groups. For organics, the relationship between export prices and production costs (WPIs) shows a small but steady rise in profit margins during this time despite a general downtrend in export prices. For plastics, profit margins remained steady throughout period; though export prices rose, the rise did not exceed the increase in production costs. For these two products, U.S. exporters' profit margins appear to guide export price patterns rather than a desire to maintain price competitiveness and market share in the face of the rising dollar.

The pattern was quite different for inorganic chemicals. Here, the U.S. export price declined sharply over the period, both in absolute terms and relative to production costs, indicating that exporters were attempting to offset at least some of the dollar's appreciation and maintain price competitiveness in overseas markets.

Dollar Depreciation Period, Early 1985-1986 --After the dollar began to depreciate, dollar export prices initially declined (for organics and plastics) or held relatively steady (inorganics) and profit margins for all three also declined. However, by 1986 profit margins for all three commodities began to rise, indicating that U.S. exporters were not allowing the depreciation effect on their overseas price competitiveness to be maximized.

Table CHEM-2

Export Prices and Profit Margins 1/
(Index Jan.-Mar. 1981=100)

Chemicals, total	1981	1982	1983	1984	1st Qtr. 1985	1985	1986[2]	4th Qtr. 1986[3]
Unit Value	101.2	99.2	101.6	104.7	102.0	98.4	99.9	102.3
Organics								
Unit Value	102.2	96.3	96.8	100.5	94.1	94.4	90.8	93.5
WPI	103.6	96.3	94.6	94.2	91.2	91.8	85.9	83.7
Profit Margins	98.7	100.0	102.3	106.7	103.2	102.8	105.9	111.7
Inorganics								
Unit Value	98.7	103.6	89.9	86.5	83.3	86.7	89.5	95.7
WPI	104.2	111.9	106.4	105.5	108.1	108.2	106.6	106.3
Profit Margins	94.8	92.6	84.5	82.0	77.0	80.1	83.9	90.0
Plastics								
Unit Value	103.3	102.2	104.6	112.4	109.3	102.7	102.8	102.0
WPI	104.5	102.4	105.3	111.5	110.6	110.1	107.1	106.3
Profit Margins	98.9	99.8	99.3	100.8	98.8	93.2	95.9	96.0
Other chemicals								
Unit Value	98.3	98.7	110.7	110.3	113.9	104.8	115.4	119.4

1/ Ratio of unit value index to wholesale price index. Index values greater than 100 indicate that unit values are rising more rapidly or falling less rapidly than production costs (WPI) and therefore profit margins are rising compared to the base period. Index values less than 100 indicate falling profit margins.
2/ January-November 1986.
3/ October-November 1986.

BASIC MANUFACTURES

Product Sample

As shown in Table BAS-1 the number of commodities included for b
manufactures was 27. Commodity groups included both 7-digit Sch
groups and BLS groups. These commodities accounted for nearly
one-third of all U.S. exports of basic manufactures in 1985.
Several broad commodity groups were not covered by the survey du
the lack of data on prices or unit values. The excluded broad
commodities included cork and wood manufactures, most nonmetalli
mineral manufactures other than glass, and manufactures of metal
other than hand tools.

Table BAS-1

Profile of Product Sample

Product 1/	Number of Products in Sample	1985 Sample Value and % of Samp. Total		Sample Share of Total U.S Exports of Product (%)
		$ mill.	(%)	
Basic Mfgs., total (6)	27*	$5,160.6	(100)	36.8%
Leather (61)	1*	$ 465.8	(9)	100.0%
Tires (62)	1*	$ 342.9	(7)	100.0%
Paper (64)	4	$ 935.4	(18)	40.2%
Textiles (65)	4*	$ 712.0	(14)	30.1%
Glass (664)	1	$ 77.5	(2)	15.4%
Iron & Steel (67)	2*	$ 256.6	(5)	20.8%
Nonferrous Metals (68)	6	$ 982.2	(19)	54.6%
Hand Tools (695)	2*	$ 686.0	(13)	100.0%
Other	6	$ 702.2	(14)	16.4%

1/ Product names are shortened versions of the full Sch. E
   descriptions. The Sch. E category's numeric designation
   represented by the products in the sample is shown
   in parentheses.
* Includes one or more BLS export price category.
Note: Totals may not add due to rounding.

Price and Profit Margin Behavior

Overall, prices of basic manufactures showed little change betwee
1981 and 1986 (Table BAS-2). Price behavior for many of the
commodity groups, however, was quite different from the overall
average.

Dollar Appreciation Period, 1981-early 1985 -- Price and profit
margin behavior for the individual commodities varied widely. At
the peak of the dollar's appreciation in early 1985, profit margi
for paper, glass, and nonferrous metals were much lower than in 1
indicating that exporters were attempting to minimize the effect

the dollar's appreciation on their export sales. The decline in export prices for glass and nonferrous metals more than offset changes in production costs (as measured by the WPI). For paper, although export prices rose slightly, the increase was far less rapid than that of production costs.

In contrast, export prices for textiles and for iron and steel climbed considerably during this period. For textiles, the increase in export price resulted in increased profit margins. For steel, profit margins also rose early in this period but later declined.

Dollar Depreciation Period, Early 1985-1986 -- Export prices and profit margins, with a few exceptions, showed little change during the early stages of the dollar's fall in 1985. In 1986, however, prices and/or profit margins generally increased considerably. It may be that U.S. exporters, seeing their competitors' prices rise relative to their own, took that as an opportunity to raise prices and profit margins, which for several product groups were squeezed considerably when the dollar was strong. Therefore, it does not appear that the full effects of the dollar's depreciation were being allowed to be passed through.

Table BAS-2

Export Prices and Profit Margins 1/
(Index Jan.-Mar. 1981=100)

	1981	1982	1983	1984	1st Qtr. 1985	1985	1986 2/	4 Q 1
Basic Mfgs., total								
Unit Value	101.4	97.7	96.7	97.5	96.9	98.1	101.2	
Leather								
Unit Value	97.1	86.1	86.8	101.2	102.9	98.5	103.6	1
WPI	101.4	98.7	97.6	97.2	95.8	95.6	97.2	
Profit Margins	95.8	87.2	89.0	104.0	107.4	103.1	106.6	1
Paper								
Unit Value	106.3	105.3	96.4	102.8	101.5	104.9	112.6	1
WPI	102.6	108.2	111.7	119.3	122.7	122.6	125.6	1
Profit Margins	103.6	97.4	86.3	86.1	82.7	85.6	89.6	8
Textiles								
Unit Value	102.3	107.0	114.0	112.6	120.7	115.5	123.4	1
WPI	101.3	104.0	104.7	104.0	103.2	103.3	103.2	1
Profit Margins	101.0	102.9	108.9	108.3	117.0	111.9	119.6	1
Glass								
Unit Value	107.5	101.9	100.5	93.5	89.7	82.5	88.5	9
WPI	101.5	105.9	106.4	107.1	110.8	109.5	110.3	1
Profit Margins	106.0	96.3	94.5	87.4	81.0	75.3	80.2	8
Iron & Steel								
Unit Value	105.0	110.0	111.5	110.3	111.6	112.7	112.3	1
WPI	102.8	104.4	105.7	109.9	110.0	109.4	105.6	1
Profit Margins	102.2	105.4	105.4	100.4	101.4	103.1	106.4	1
Nonferrous Metals								
Unit Value	96.1	81.8	85.6	86.8	77.2	79.0	80.9	7
WPI	99.0	91.3	95.6	96.0	91.3	90.9	90.0	9
Profit Margins	97.0	89.6	89.5	90.4	84.5	86.9	90.0	8
Tires								
Unit Value	104.0	104.1	99.5	99.8	100.6	98.7	99.1	9
WPI	102.6	104.4	100.4	99.1	97.8	97.2	95.9	9
Profit Margins	101.3	99.7	99.1	100.7	102.8	101.6	103.4	10
Hand Tools								
Unit Value	111.5	107.5	113.5	100.0	101.9	118.6	105.9	9
WPI	101.3	105.3	108.7	110.9	112.6	113.7	114.6	11
Profit Margins	110.0	102.1	104.4	90.2	90.5	104.2	92.4	7

1/ Ratio of Unit value index to wholesale price index. Index values greater than 100 indicate that unit values are risi[ng] more rapidly or falling less rapidly than production costs and therefore profit margins are rising compared to the ba[se] period. Index values less than 100 indicate falling profi[t] margins.

2/ January-November 1986.

3/ October-November 1986.

MISCELLANEOUS MANUFACTURES

Product Sample

As shown in Table MISC-1, the product sample for miscellaneous
manufactures totalled 8. The sample included both 7-digit Sch. E
numbers as well as BLS export price categories. The commodities
included here accounted for more than half of all U.S. exports in
the miscellaneous manufactures class.

Table MISC-1

Profile of Product Sample

Product 1/	Number of Products in Sample	1985 Sample Value and % of Samp. Total $ mill.	(%)	Sample Share of Total U.S. Exports of Product (%)
Misc. Mfgs., total (8)	8*	$ 8,722.5	(100)	56.9%
Instruments (87)	1*	$ 6,505.2	(75)	100.0%
Photo Supp. (882)	3	$ 613.7	(7)	46.7%
Plastic Articles (891x)	1	$ 1,246.7	(14)	100.0%
Other	3	$ 356.9	(4)	5.7%

1/ Product names are shortened versions of the full Sch. E
   descriptions. The Sch. E category's numeric designation
   represented by the products in the sample is shown
   in parentheses.
* Includes one or more BLS export price category.
Note: Totals may not add due to rounding.

Price and Profit Margin Behavior

U.S. export prices in this category showed sizable increases between
1981 and 1986 (Table MISC-2). This was largely due to the
instruments group, which carries a heavy relative weight.

Dollar Appreciation Period, 1981-early 1985 -- Prices and profit
margins behaved quite differently for the three commodities included
here. For instruments, export prices rose sharply, outstripping the
sizable increase in production costs (as measured by the WPI) so
that profit margins rose slightly (Table MISC-2). Export prices of
plastic articles also increased, but at about the same rate as
production costs so that profit margins declined marginally. U.S.
exporters of instruments and plastic articles did not appear to
minimize increases in dollar export prices to offset the dollar's
appreciation.

In contrast, for photographic supplies, export prices declined
significantly during the dollar appreciation period despite
increased production costs. Thus, profit margins for photo supplies
were squeezed considerably. Here, it appears that U.S. exporters
tried to offset at least part of the dollar's appreciation and
maintain price competitiveness and market shares.

Dollar Depreciation Period, Early 1985-1986 -- Export prices for
three commodities have risen since the dollar began to depreciate
early 1986. Profit margins, especially for photo supplies, also
grew during this period. Thus, U.S. exporters do not appear to h
allowed the full dollar depreciation to be passed through in terms
of the foreign currency prices of their goods. For instruments,
profit margins and prices simply continued their upward trend of t
earlier period. For plastic articles, prices rose in 1986 after
being virtually unchanged for several years, and profit margins al
grew. Prices and profit margins for photo supplies also increased
in contrast with their behavior when the dollar was appreciating
indicating an attempt to recoup the decline in profit margins
evident before 1985.

Table MISC-2

Export Prices and Profit Margins 1/
(Index Jan.-Mar. 1981=100)

	1981	1982	1983	1984	1st Qtr. 1985	1985	1986 2/
Misc. Mfgs., total							
Unit Value	102.6	110.6	115.3	117.4	118.3	119.3	124.1
Instruments							
Unit Value	103.4	113.9	119.8	122.2	124.1	125.8	129.9
WPI	103.5	110.2	115.4	119.5	121.3	121.0	123.2
Profit Margins	99.9	103.4	103.8	102.2	102.6	103.7	105.4
Plastic Articles							
Unit Value	102.6	106.8	107.3	109.7	109.1	109.5	114.2
WPI	102.4	105.4	107.8	111.2	111.4	111.1	111.9
Profit Margins	100.2	101.3	99.5	98.7	97.9	98.5	102.1
Photo Supplies							
Unit Value	97.3	97.7	94.5	97.9	93.9	87.1	98.9
WPI	99.9	99.5	103.1	105.6	105.8	106.8	108.7
Profit Margins	97.5	98.2	91.6	92.7	88.5	81.6	90.9

1/ Ratio of Unit value index to wholesale price index. Ind
   values greater than 100 indicate that unit values are ris
   more rapidly or falling less rapidly than production cost
   and therefore profit margins are rising compared to the b
   period. Index values less than 100 indicate falling prof
   margins.
2/ January-November 1986.
3/ October-November 1986.

MACHINERY

Product Sample

As shown in Table MACH-1, the number of commodities included in the sample for machinery was 62. Commodity groups included both 7-digit Sch. E groups and BLS groups. Overall, the coverage in machinery, in terms of the portion of total exports represented by the sample is high, in large part for the inclusion of many BLS commodity groups which are more aggregate than the Sch. E commodity groups.

Table MACH-1

Profile of Product Sample

Product 1/	Number of Products in Sample	1985 Sample Value and % of Samp. $ mill.	Total (%)	Sample Share of Total U.S. Exports of Product (%)
Machinery, total (7 ex. 78,79)	62*	$41,783.3	(100)	70.2%
Piston Engines (713)	5*	$ 3,455.5	(8)	82.6%
Non-piston Engines (714)	4	$ 1,149.4	(3)	32.0%
Elec. Motors etc. (716)	1*	$ 764.5	(2)	100.0%
Ag. Mach. ex. tractors (721)	2*	$ 854.3	(2)	100.0%
Tractors, non-road (722)	3	$ 266.7	(1)	35.7%
Contractors Equip. (723)	2*	$ 3,438.2	(8)	84.3%
Metalworking Mach. Tools (736)	1*	$ 869.3	(2)	100.0%
Heat./Cool. Equip. (741)	1*	$ 1,790.5	(4)	100.0%
Pumps (742,743)	2*	$ 2,219.2	(5)	100.0%
Ball/Rollers, Bearings (7491)	1*	$ 304.8	(1)	100.0%
Taps, Cocks, Valves (7492)	1*	$ 610.4	(1)	100.0%
Office Machines (751)	4	$ 281.3	(1)	56.1%
ADP Mach. & Equip. (752)	9	$ 6,964.6	(17)	98.0%
Office, ADP Mach. Pts. (759)	1*	$ 7,322.5	(18)	100.0%
Telecommunications Equip. (764)	3*	$ 3,747.3	(9)	100.0%
Current Carrying Dev. (772)	3*	$ 2,196.3	(5)	100.0%
Electro-Medical App. (7741)	1*	$ 891.9	(2)	100.0%
Elec. Components (776)	9	$ 1,009.4	(2)	21.8%
Other	9*	$ 3,647.2	(9)	27.8%

1/ Product names are shortened versions of the full Sch. E descriptions. The Sch. E category's numeric description represented by the products in the sample is shown in parentheses.
* Includes one or more BLS export price category.
Note: Totals may not add due to rounding.

Price and Profit Margin Behavior

On average, export prices for machinery rose moderately during both the period of dollar appreciation and depreciation periods (Table

MACH-2). The average, however, masks considerable diversity among
product groups. Export prices of some products rose substantiall
while for others, notably electronic components and ADP equipment
export prices declined.

Dollar Appreciation Period, 1981-early 1985 -- Export prices for
virtually all machinery products covered in this survey climbed
during the period when the dollar was appreciating, at least
initially (Table MACH-2). As a result, given the large dollar
appreciation during this period, the price competitiveness of U.S.
exports relative to foreign suppliers probably declined
considerably. Two important exceptions to this pattern were in AI
machines and equipment and electronic components, where export uni
values declined sharply. In addition, export prices for contracto
equipment, heating & cooling equipment, and for ball/roller bearir
all leveled off in mid-1982 after increasing initially.

The behavior of profit margins was quite different among the varic
machinery products surveyed here. For half the products, profit
margins on exports showed little if any change during the dollar
depreciation period. Profit margins for non-piston engines, pumps
and office machines, however, rose considerably as increases in
export prices were much stronger than changes in production costs.
In contrast, profit margins declined for several products: electr:
motors, heating/cooling equip., ADP machines, parts of office and
ADP machines, and electronic components. For the latter three
commodities, the profit margin declines were substantial.

Dollar Depreciation Period, Early 1985-1986 -- During this period,
export prices for more than half the commodities increased. This
was true for both commodities, ADP machines and electronic
components, where unit values in the dollar appreciation period ha
fallen with both experiencing declining profit margins. For both
these products, profit margins in the dollar depreciation period
increased. In general, however, profit margins for most of the
commodities showed little, if any, change.

Table MACH-2

Export Prices and Profit Margins 1/
(Index Jan.-Mar. 1981=100)

	1981	1982	1983	1984	1st Qtr. 1985	1985	1986 2/	4th Qtr. 1986 3/
Machinery, total								
Unit Value	102.5	106.1	108.3	110.5	109.0	111.5	111.5	115.0
Piston Engines								
Unit Value	103.0	107.4	111.9	116.8	117.9	119.6	123.5	128.2
WPI	103.1	109.2	112.2	114.8	116.5	117.0	118.8	119.3
Profit Margins	99.9	98.4	99.7	101.8	101.2	102.2	104.0	107.5
Non-piston Engines								
Unit Value	110.9	117.4	174.3	204.7	155.9	188.2	184.8	175.6
WPI	103.1	109.2	112.2	114.8	116.5	117.0	118.8	119.3
Profit Margins	107.5	107.4	155.3	178.4	133.8	160.8	155.6	147.2
Electric Motors etc.								
Unit Value	103.0	109.4	108.6	109.1	110.2	114.2	118.1	122.6
WPI	103.1	107.8	114.7	118.4	121.8	122.2	121.6	119.6
Profit Margins	99.9	101.4	94.7	92.2	90.4	93.4	97.2	102.5
Ag. Mach. ex. tractors								
Unit Value	102.6	110.5	119.2	122.5	126.3	125.0	119.5	117.2
WPI	102.8	110.7	116.0	119.6	120.9	120.9	121.7	121.9
Profit Margins	99.8	99.8	102.7	102.4	104.4	103.4	98.2	96.1
Tractors, non-road								
Unit Value	107.7	123.4	126.5	127.7	127.1	132.3	132.3	133.4
WPI	104.6	113.0	118.0	120.9	122.0	121.6	122.1	122.4
Profit Margins	102.9	109.2	107.2	105.6	104.2	108.9	108.4	109.0
Contractors Equip.								
Unit Value	105.6	114.2	112.7	114.9	114.5	115.2	114.3	112.9
WPI	103.6	111.1	113.7	115.3	117.1	117.1	118.5	119.0
Profit Margins	101.9	102.8	99.1	99.7	97.7	98.4	96.5	94.8
Metalworking Mach. Tools								
Unit Value	103.4	111.0	113.9	116.1	117.9	120.1	123.8	125.7
WPI	103.1	109.9	111.8	114.4	116.2	117.1	119.1	119.7
Profit Margins	100.3	101.0	101.9	101.6	101.5	102.6	103.9	105.0
Heat./Cool. Equipment								
Unit Value	102.4	107.7	107.7	107.5	106.7	107.9	109.6	110.3
WPI	101.9	106.3	110.1	111.5	112.8	113.6	115.0	115.2
Profit Margins	100.5	101.4	97.8	96.5	94.6	95.0	95.3	95.7
Pumps								
Unit Value	104.8	113.6	115.1	123.7	130.2	130.4	132.1	133.3
WPI	104.0	111.3	111.3	112.0	113.6	114.2	115.9	116.6
Profit Margins	100.8	102.1	103.4	110.4	114.6	114.2	114.0	114.3

1/ Ratio of Unit value index to wholesale price index. Index values greater than 100 indicate that unit values are rising more rapidly or falling less rapidly than production costs (WPI) and therefore profit margins are rising compared to the base period. Index values less than 100 indicate falling profit margins.

2/ January-November 1986.

3/ October-November 1986.

Table MACH-2 (continued)

Export Prices and Profit Margins 1/
(Index Jan.-Mar. 1981=100)

	1981	1982	1983	1984	1st Qtr. 1985	1985	1986 2/	4th Qtr. 1986 3/
Ball/Rollers, Bearings								
Unit Value	103.4	113.3	113.4	112.2	113.5	114.3	117.8	119.0
WPI	104.8	114.0	114.1	117.3	119.1	120.7	122.4	122.6
Profit Margins	98.7	99.4	99.4	95.6	95.3	94.7	96.3	97.0
Taps, Cocks, Valves								
Unit Value	102.9	111.0	117.2	121.3	123.3	124.7	128.9	132.5
WPI	103.1	109.2	112.2	114.8	116.5	117.0	118.8	119.3
Profit Margins	99.8	101.6	104.5	105.7	105.8	106.5	108.5	111.1
Office Machines								
Unit Value	129.7	183.1	268.8	227.5	172.9	179.7	95.1	115.1
WPI	101.1	104.0	105.8	105.6	105.4	105.7	106.0	106.3
Profit Margins	128.1	175.9	253.9	215.3	164.1	170.0	89.7	108.2
ADP Mach. & Equipment								
Unit Value	100.1	87.5	65.3	54.2	59.6	63.6	62.6	63.6
WPI	102.9	108.3	112.3	116.3	118.5	118.7	120.5	121.1
Profit Margins	97.3	80.9	58.2	46.6	50.3	53.6	52.0	52.5
Office, ADP Mach. Parts								
Unit Value	101.1	101.8	102.7	100.4	100.3	99.8	100.0	99.7
WPI	102.9	108.3	112.3	116.3	118.5	118.7	120.5	121.1
Profit Margins	98.2	94.1	91.5	86.3	84.7	84.1	83.0	82.3
Telecommunications Equip.								
Unit Value	102.3	108.3	113.8	115.8	141.1	128.1	121.3	122.3
WPI	102.9	108.3	112.3	116.3	118.5	118.7	120.5	121.1
Profit Margins	99.4	100.0	101.4	99.6	119.0	107.9	100.7	101.0
Current Carrying Wiring Devices								
Unit Value	103.0	112.0	111.5	115.1	128.6	132.0	138.9	144.7
WPI	104.8	113.3	117.2	123.5	126.1	126.5	131.1	132.6
Profit Margins	98.2	98.8	95.2	93.1	102.0	104.4	105.9	109.2
Electro-Medical Apparatus								
Unit Value	103.3	107.8	110.8	110.8	111.4	109.8	109.6	110.1
WPI	102.9	108.3	112.3	116.3	118.5	118.7	120.5	121.1
Profit Margins	100.4	99.6	98.7	95.3	94.0	92.5	91.0	90.9
Electronic Components								
Unit Value	88.4	82.0	78.8	70.0	86.2	83.6	85.2	87.7
WPI	102.0	106.8	111.4	117.3	120.6	120.1	122.4	123.4
Profit Margins	86.8	76.8	70.8	59.7	71.5	69.6	69.6	71.1

1/ Ratio of Unit value index to wholesale price index. Index values greater than 100 indicate that unit values are rising more rapidly or falling less rapidly than production costs (WPI) and therefore profit margins are rising compared to the base period. Index values less than 100 indicate falling profit margins.

2/ January-November 1986.

3/ October-November 1986.

TRANSPORTATION EQUIPMENT

Product Sample

As shown in Table TRANS-1, the number of commodities included in the sample for transportation equipment was 15. Commodity groups included both 7-digit Sch. E groups and BLS groups. Overall, the coverage, in terms of the portion of total exports represented by the sample was high and was never less than 50 percent for any of the individual commodity groups.

Table TRANS-1

Profile of Product Sample

Product 1/	Number of Products in Sample	1985 Sample Value and % of Samp. Total		Sample Share of Total U.S. Exports of Product (%)
		$ mill.	(%)	
Transport Equip. (78,79)	15*	$29,358.3	(100)	84.4%
Passenger Cars (781)	2	$ 5,995.8	(20)	98.2%
Trucks (7821)	3	$ 1,437.6	(5)	70.9%
Special Purpose Veh. (7822)	1	$ 136.0	(1)	56.9%
Motor Vehicle Parts (784)	2*	$10,764.3	(37)	100.0%
Rail Locomotives, etc. (7916)	1	$ 146.3	(1)	98.1%
Airplanes (7925)	5	$ 5,298.0	(18)	64.3%
Air/Spacecraft Parts (7929)	1*	$ 5,580.3	(19)	100.0%

1/ Product names are shortened versions of the full Sch. E descriptions. The Sch. E category's numeric designation represented by the products in the sample is shown in parentheses.
* Includes one or more BLS export price category.
Note: Totals may not add due to rounding.

Price and Profit Margin Behavior

Dollar Appreciation Period, 1981-early 1985 -- Both prices and profit margins for most of the transportation categories included in the survey increased during the dollar appreciation period (Table TRANS-2).

Dollar Depreciation Period, early 1985-1986 -- After the dollar began to depreciate, export prices for three of the transportation products continued to rise: aircraft parts, passenger cars, and trucks. Profit margins, on the other hand, levelled off or declined in all products except for passenger cars.

Table TRANS-2

Export Prices and Profit Margins 1/
(Index Jan.-Mar. 1981=100)

	1981	1982	1983	1984	1st Qtr. 1985	1985	1986 2/
Transport Equip., Total							
Unit Value	104.9	117.1	126.9	131.0	128.2	132.8	138.2
Passenger Cars							
Unit Value	106.6	115.6	118.3	124.6	131.7	134.1	149.3
WPI	103.2	107.3	109.6	111.6	114.4	114.7	118.5
Profit Margins	103.2	107.7	108.0	111.7	115.2	116.9	126.2
Trucks							
Unit Value	102.9	111.3	112.6	112.3	117.8	118.4	124.9
WPI	103.9	109.4	112.3	116.8	121.9	122.8	129.2
Profit Margins	99.0	101.6	100.3	96.2	96.6	96.5	96.8
Special Purpose Vehicles							
Unit Value	107.9	121.9	123.5	160.7	116.8	154.5	158.8
WPI	103.4	108.4	111.0	113.5	116.3	116.8	120.9
Profit Margins	104.2	112.6	110.0	141.7	100.5	132.7	131.8
Motor Vehicle Parts							
Unit Value	102.6	110.0	113.8	119.6	119.6	120.3	121.2
WPI	103.4	108.4	111.0	113.5	116.3	116.8	120.9
Profit Margins	99.3	101.5	102.6	105.4	102.9	103.0	100.3
Rail Locomotives, etc.							
Unit Value	88.4	119.5	135.1	138.5	41.8	40.6	29.3
WPI	100.1	101.1	102.6	103.5	102.9	103.8	105.3
Profit Margins	88.3	118.3	131.7	133.7	40.6	39.2	27.8
Aircraft							
Unit Value	106.7	130.0	165.3	158.9	129.3	147.5	152.0
WPI	100.4	101.8	107.1	108.3	108.3	109.4	117.3
Profit Margins	106.2	127.7	154.2	146.7	119.4	134.8	129.8
Air/Spacecraft Parts							
Unit Value	105.8	120.5	127.3	135.7	140.4	143.3	148.8
WPI	100.4	101.8	107.1	108.3	108.3	109.4	117.3
Profit Margins	105.4	118.4	118.8	125.3	129.6	131.0	126.9

1/ Ratio of Unit value index to wholesale price index. Ind
values greater than 100 indicate that unit values are ri
more rapidly or falling less rapidly than production cos
and therefore profit margins are rising compared to the l
period. Index values less than 100 indicate falling pro
margins.

2/ January-November 1986.

3/ Octover-November 1986.

SUMMARY AND CONCLUSIONS

SUMMARY

The evidence obtained from the approximately 40 products detailed in this sample indicates that during the dollar appreciation period, U.S. exporters generally did not attempt to maintain their competitiveness in foreign markets either by lowering price or by cutting profit margins. After the dollar began to depreciate in early 1985, exporters generally did allow the positive effects of the depreciation on competitiveness to occur as they did not expand profit margins, although export prices increased or held steady in most cases (Figure 2).

Figure 2

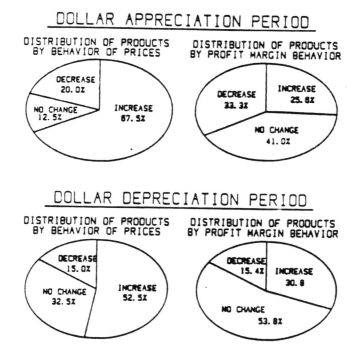

Dollar Appreciation Period

During the dollar appreciation period of 1981-1985:Q1, export prices for more than three-quarters of the products either rose or held even. On average, prices rose by about 15 percent during this period. In addition to these price increases, the U.S. dollar appreciated about 25 percent in real terms. These two factors taken together indicate that for most products, U.S. exporters experienced a significant decline in price competitiveness. In addition, at the peak of the dollar's appreciation, profit margins for two-thirds of

the included products were either unchanged or larger than in 198
Thus, with a few exceptions, listed below, U.S. exporters do not
appear to have attempted to minimize the loss in price
competitiveness vis-a-vis foreign suppliers that resulted from th
dollar's appreciation. The following summary indicates those
products where profit margins did show definite declines during t
dollar appreciation period:

> Chemicals -- inorganic chemicals
> Basic Manufactures -- paper, glass, nonferrous metals, hand
> tools
> Miscellaneous Manufactures -- photographic supplies
> Machinery -- ADP equipment, ADP parts, electronic component
> electric motors, electro-medical apparatus
> Transportation Equipment -- None.

Dollar Depreciation Period

After the dollar began to depreciate (after the first quarter of
1985), export prices increased for half of the products in the
survey and remained unchanged from their first quarter 1985 level
an additional one-third of the products. The average price incre
for all products was 5.5 percent. Not surprisingly, decreases in
profit margins were much less frequent than during the period whe
the dollar was appreciating. In all the broad commodity groups
except transportation equipment, the number of product groups in
which profit margins declined were fewer than during the dollar
appreciation period. The following summary shows products whose
where profit margins showed a definite increase after the dollar
began to depreciate:

> o Chemicals -- organic chemicals, inorganic chemicals;
> o Basic Manufactures -- leather, paper products, textiles,
> glass;
> o Miscellaneous Manufactures -- photographic supplies
> o Machinery -- electric motors;
> o Transport Equipment -- none

CONCLUSIONS

Many U.S. exporters have failed to adjust to exchange rate change
so as to maintain export sales and/or market shares. The failure
prices and profit margins to decline when the dollar was strong
indicates that U.S. firms generally seek to maintain profit
margins. That profit margins did not generally increase when the
dollar fell probably indicates a continuation of the pattern of
maintaining profit margins rather than an effort to obtain the
maximum competitive benefits of the weaker dollar. It should be
noted that when the dollar is depreciating, it is possible both t
improve profit margins and to gain at least partial competitive
price benefits.

There is some historical evidence to support this conclusion. Data on ratios of exports to total shipments collected for more than three-quarters of the sample product groups included in this study generally show that when the dollar is strong, exports decline as a share of total shipments -- exports grow more slowly than domestic shipments or in many cases actually decline in value. This may reflect the reduced price competitiveness of exports and the general unwillingness of U.S. exporters to cut prices and profit margins to maintain foreign sales. In contrast, when the dollar is weak, exports increase as a share of total shipments, because although exporters maintain profit margins, the weaker dollar partly offsets any price increases and price competitiveness improves. There may be several reason for the apparent lack of response to exchange rate changes on the part of U.S. firms:

1. Exports are sometimes a small part of total shipments for U.S. firms operating in the huge U.S. domestic market that they are viewed only as a residual. While this may be true in some cases, available data indicate that for some product groups, exports constitute upwards of 10% and 20% of total shipments.

2. A sizable part of U.S. exports are viewed as "unique" products which are therefore relatively insensitive to price. While some products probably are "unique", this is probably becoming less frequent, as is suggested by the turn from strong surplus to deficit in the mid-1980s for high technology goods. The competition for the products of our smokestack industries from Japan, Europe, and the newly industrializing countries has spread into "unique" high technology products as well.

3. Many major U.S. exporters are large multinationals with subsidiaries and production facilities worldwide. Their overall profitability therefore does not depend solely on their exports from U.S. based facilities but rather on how effectively they allocate sales and production and adjust the prices of products among their overseas and U.S. facilities.

4. U.S. firms may have been hesitant to lower profit margins when the dollar was strong due to concerns about dumping charges by foreign countries.